Dogs
for Life

Published by Rily Publications Ltd, 2020
ISBN 978-1-84967-415-7
Copyright © Alison Stokes, 2020

The Quick Reads project in Wales is an initiative coordinated by the
Books Council of Wales and supported by the Welsh Government.
Printed and bound by CPI Group (UK) Ltd, Croydon, CR0 4YY

Cover design by Tanwen Haf

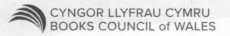

CYNGOR LLYFRAU CYMRU
BOOKS COUNCIL of WALES

Dogs for Life

ALISON STOKES

Foreword

Animals have always been part of my life. I am interested in the ways that animals and humans can benefit each other, and this has guided me throughout my career.

In my school holidays and during winter weekends from the age of 13 I worked on a small dairy farm near my home in Ayrshire, Scotland. I learned a lot, doing everything from milking cows to mucking out hens and helping with hay making. After I qualified as a vet I moved to Carmarthenshire to work in a vet practice that looked after mostly large farm animals, although I did sometimes treat sick cats and dogs.

It didn't take long for me to realise that although drugs could relieve most common health problems of pets such as skin disease or ear infection, when the drugs stopped the problem came back. I wanted to be able to do more.

At about that time, I read an article about acupuncture.

It was the mid-1970s and I heard how some doctors in Europe were using the ancient Chinese method of placing needles at certain points in a patient's body to stimulate nerves and muscles. It was seen as a new, alternative way of treating disease without having to take so many drugs. I decided to learn more and qualified to become a human acupuncturist. At the same time, this led me to find out more about other complementary therapies. One of these was macrobiotics, which took the view that many modern human illnesses such as heart disease, diabetes, mental illness, cancers and other degenerative diseases were a result of our way of eating. Our modern Western-style diet consists mainly of meat, dairy foods, sugars and chemicals instead of the more traditional diets of our forbears which were based around grains and vegetables, seeds and fruits. This was the root of many of our modern diseases. This completely changed the way I thought about what I ate, and I became a fan of health promotion rather than disease treatment.

I began to introduce this method of eating into my work to bring changes into the way I was treating sick animals. I thought that if this way of eating could benefit humans, why not pets? When owners brought their animals into my vet practice, I would use medication as a short-term fix but as a way of preventing the illness coming back, I would suggest a change in diet. My advice was to feed a home-cooked diet of brown rice, vegetables and meat. At that time, good quality organic brown rice was difficult to buy in west Wales (in some places it still is), so the practice stocked and sold rice for pet owners. In other practices, pet owners came in for wormers or medicines and tablets; in our surgery they came to buy brown rice! We saw fantastic improvements in the health of dogs (and even cats) when they were fed this type of natural diet. Skin, ear and digestive problems cleared up, never to return.

Most of my customers, however, did not have the time to cook for their pets so the idea of producing food they could buy was born. Burns Real Food for Dogs was launched in 1993 and the rest, as they say, is history.

Today, as the founder and owner of the successful Burns Pet Nutrition Limited business which sells pet food all over the world, I am in a position to use my company's profits to help animals and their humans too.

I set up the Burns Pet Nutrition Foundation in 2006. When a customer buys Burns pet food, a portion of the cost is put back into the community. We run projects that help children to read, host coffee mornings for older people and work with people who have brain injuries.

Today, the John Burns Foundation employs 9 members of staff and has a sister charity in Ireland. Our aim is very simple, and that is to make a difference to the lives of people and their animals. At our headquarters in Kidwelly we run community gardens and arts and craft workshops, where people who feel lonely can come and learn new skills and enjoy themselves.

One of our projects is the Burns By Your Side children's reading scheme. Poor literacy is a huge problem in the UK: one in six children struggle to read, and 12 million adults have the reading levels of an 11-year-old. At Burns we want to change literacy levels for the next generation by improving children's confidence in reading with the help of canine companions.

Burns By Your Side was launched in 2015 and is active across west and south Wales and has also started in Ireland. We have over 70 qualified volunteer and dog teams in schools, colleges, libraries and other educational settings.

When these specially trained dogs (and their owners) come to hear children read, it's fun. And that makes all the difference. Learning to read is often about overcoming fears rather than intellectual limitations. Animals are ideal reading companions because they:

→   Help children to relax
→   Listen attentively
→   Do not judge, laugh, or criticise
→   Allow children to read at their own pace
→   Make a session less scary than reading out loud
     to the class.

We are delighted that some of the dogs and their owners who are part of our scheme have shared their stories in this wonderful book, along with some other truly inspiring stories about dogs, their people and the incredible roles they play in our lives.

I defy anyone to read this book with a dry eye!

John Burns,
Founder, Burns Pet Nutrition, Kidwelly.

Contents

Introduction

For centuries humans have shared a special bond with their animals. As a nation of dog lovers it's not hard to see how our pets can provide comfort and friendship and lift our spirits when we are down.

Dogs, however, are more than man's best friend. They are also man's greatest ally. Women's too!

The idea of dogs being trained to provide support and service is not new. The history books are full of stories of brave hounds helping humans. If you walk along the promenade in Swansea you will find a memorial to the Welsh black retriever known as Swansea Jack. This canine hero is remembered for the way he rescued 27 sailors from the docks and riverbanks of Swansea.

A visit to the small village of Beddgelert in Snowdonia, north Wales, will bring you to the tomb of Gelert and the ultimate yet tragic story of canine loyalty. For more than 800 years, legends have told how Gelert, the faithful hound of Welsh Prince Llywelyn, gave his life to protect the Prince's baby son from a wolf attack.

For over a century, dogs have been trained to do important, life-saving work in places that are too difficult or dangerous for humans. During the First World War, dogs such as Airedale terriers, lurchers, retrievers and sheepdogs were trained to go undercover. Running across all terrains in darkness, they relayed important messages to soldiers fighting in the trenches, which they carried in little tins on their collars. Dogs were also used to sniff out wounded soldiers and carry medical supplies and water during battle.

During the Second World War, more than 7,000 pet dogs were sent by their owners to be trained for war. Dispatched all over the world, these loyal companions boosted morale and saved many lives. The use of dogs in war zones continues in recent times with teams of dogs and their handlers trained to detect bombs, guns and Taliban terrorists in Afghanistan.

Dogs also play an important role in law enforcement, helping the police to search for drugs and explosives, to find missing people or crime scene evidence, or to bring down criminals.

Today, the use of dogs to provide medical support and companionship has grown. One of the oldest, best-known services, Guide Dogs, has been training dogs to be the eyes of their human partners since the 1930s. In other areas, dogs can be taught to be the ears of their hearing-impaired or deaf owners. By touching their feet with their paws they can alert them to sounds such as the telephone ringing or alarms going off.

Assistance and service dogs can be trained to help disabled people with many everyday jobs, for example, to fetch phones in emergencies, empty washing machines or take off a person's coat or jacket. For these people their dogs are more than just pets, they are a lifeline.

Children with autism can also benefit from the huge range of practical and emotional support that a trained therapy dog can give. Autism is a sensory disability which makes everyday life challenging. As well as the practical help, organisations such as Dogs for Good train animals to give close and supportive friendship that helps a child stay calm and focused.

On the medical front, dogs are now being trained as bio-detection dogs. Using their supersensitive sense of smell, they can detect diseases, such as cancer, in a person's breath or on medical samples. They can also sense tiny changes in an individual's personal odour, triggered by their disease, and alert them to an impending medical event.

Some organisations recruit pets and their owners to

visit hospitals, care homes and even prisons, where they can give comfort, joy and hope. Even dogs who were treated cruelly in their early lives show they have love to give back by providing therapy to people with disabilities and dementia. Their work in care homes can improve communication in residents by evoking memories and sparking conversation.

Here are the stories of some of these very special animals with very important jobs to do, as told to me by their owners and those who they have helped.

Heartwarming and inspiring, emotional and uplifting, *Dogs for Life* shows how some amazing animals are changing the lives of the humans who love them.

It's no surprise we call our dogs our best friends.

Alison Stokes

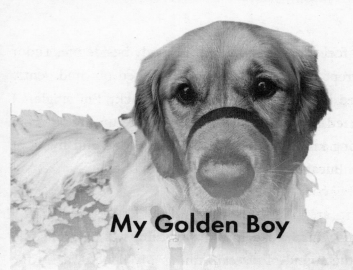

My Golden Boy

The guide dog that is better than any dating app

By Angharad Paget-Jones

The alarm went off waking me, quite rudely I thought, from the middle of a globe-trotting adventure.

My private Learjet had just touched down on the runway at New York's JFK Airport. A fancy chauffeur in a smart, charcoal grey suit and a peaked cap was holding up a sign in his white-gloved hand. It read "Welcome to New York, Miss Paget-Jones!" A stretch limousine was waiting on the tarmac, its rear door open and waiting for me to step in. Damn that alarm – I was ready to take on the Big Apple.

I rolled over onto my side and closed my eyes, hoping to rekindle the last moments of my dream. As I turned, I could feel the weight of another body beside me. Tudor had crept into my bed again. I reached out and gently stroked his silky, golden hair. "It's lucky I'm single," I muttered as Tudor ran his wet tongue up my chin – a morning kiss. I hadn't always been alone and living at home. But then, I hadn't always been blind.

* *

One morning I woke up and everything was black. I could hear the sound of water running. My fiancé was in the shower.

"Hey, who turned out all the lights?" I shouted. I wasn't too worried at first. I was born with cerebral palsy, a condition which affects the way my muscles work, so I was used to my body not working quite the way it should.

It's pretty common for people like me to have trouble seeing things, as the brain controls what we see and how we interpret it. Some people with cerebral palsy have eyes turned in or out, others have cataracts. I was one of the kids who had issues with focusing, and I experienced a loss in my field of vision.

It's estimated that one in every 400 babies born in the UK have cerebral palsy. It happens when a child's brain is damaged while it's still developing, either before, during or immediately after birth. For me, it meant that my childhood was a succession of falls and injuries, with constant plasters on knees and blushing purple-grey bruises. I would shrug it off, just thinking I was clumsier than most of the other kids in my school. What was really happening was that my brain wasn't sending out the right messages to the muscles in my legs and arms so they could work properly. Sometimes it felt like being in the wrong body.

Some people with more severe cases of cerebral palsy can't do anything for themselves and are virtually locked in their own bodies, unable to walk or talk. I considered myself lucky as I had led a pretty normal life so far, if you can call blacking out and smashing your face on the floor every now and again normal.

Still in darkness, I screwed up my eyes, and then opened them wide. I hoped that whatever cloud had descended over my sight in the night would clear. But hope is a terrible thing sometimes.

**

There had been warning signs: dizziness, nausea and severe headaches that left me incapable of doing anything except lying down in a dark room. I had ignored them, blaming the looming deadline for my final year university dissertation. I was working harder than ever to make sure I got a good grade in my journalism degree. It was my dream to start a career in the media one day. I had ambitions to report politics on the television news. I wanted to work in Parliament, be at the heart of breaking stories about Britain's laws and tax scandals. I dreamed of being on the other side of a microphone, making Prime Ministers and Presidents squirm when I asked them difficult questions. Always questioning, always wanting to know more, just like the BBC's Laura Kuenssberg – that's the career path I had in mind.

My sight did not return.

For the next few months, my vision continued to deteriorate and I was registered as partially sighted. It was a scary, bleak time and my spirits were low. You cannot imagine how it feels to lose such a taken-for-granted sense. I groped my way around the house, bumping my shins into furniture and tripping over even more than usual. Within a year, all I could see was a tiny chink of light through the centre of my left eye. On a good day it was like looking through one of those pinhole cameras that protect your eyes when you look at a solar eclipse. Most days I was completely in the dark. That's when I was registered as blind.

"Why do you want a guide dog?" my boyfriend asked me. "Everyone will be able to tell that you're blind if you've got a dog. I can be your guide."

"I want a guide dog," I insisted. "It's hard enough not being able to see ever again. Having to depend on people for the rest of my life will be a million times worse."

And as it turned out, my fiancé was not someone I could depend on. Shortly after that we split up and I was put forward as a suitable candidate for a guide dog. It was around that time that I also gave up on my dream of being a journalist. "I'm sure you can go back to it one day," my mum said on the phone, kindly. "Blind people can do almost anything these days."

"This is all so new to me," I told her. "I can't think about what I'm going to be doing in five or ten years when I can barely look after myself today."

"You'll retrain yourself," she said. "I know you will."

"But how?"

I moved back home, my confidence in tatters. I was 21 – I should have been starting my life, not going back to the beginning. Where I had once been a happy-go-lucky, sociable person, I became reclusive. I didn't like going outside the house. I was given a white cane to use to help me get around, but I hated it.

I had lived in the same village all my life. Everyone in the area knew me as Angharad, the clumsy, awkward girl, but they had never known me as blind. Now I felt that every time I walked outside using a white stick, people would look at me and whisper, "What's wrong with her? Why is she pretending to be blind?" Looking back now, I'm sure they wouldn't have been that unkind. But I was proud and finding it difficult adjusting to this new life without sight.

**

I was referred to the Guide Dogs Cymru charity, which sent someone out to meet me and check whether I was suitable to have a dog. Before I could be put on the waiting list, I needed to show them that I was fit enough to give a dog the daily walks it would need and able to care for a fully-grown, active dog. They also checked that no one in my family smoked, as second-hand smoke is harmful to dogs the same as it is to us. Having a guide dog is a great privilege but also a great responsibility. It costs £55,000 to train and look after a guide dog through its working life, so the charity has to make sure that it's going to a place where it's properly cared for. Just hearing those numbers made my spine tingle. £55,000. That's more than a deposit for a house.

"So where would you go if you had a guide dog?" the assessor asked me, drinking tea on my mother's couch. "In fact, would you be happy showing me?"

I told her I would. Together we walked to the places that I used to visit regularly before I lost my sight. We walked from my house to the bus stop and took a bus into the centre of Swansea then Cardiff, passing my favourite shops. On the way back we stopped by my local shop and park.

"My body has an unexplained and annoying way of fainting and falling over," I told her outside the park.

"That does sound rather annoying," she said, a smile in her voice.

"This is what happened last time," I said, pointing to the scars from when I had broken my nose and cheekbone and damaged my eye socket. "I missed a curb and broke my fall with my face."

The assessor went quiet and all I could hear was the creaking of the swings. I felt nervous all of a sudden that I had said too much, that admitting to these falls would mean I wasn't the best candidate for a guide dog.

"Well, due to your balance problems," she said, finally, "I recommend you get a bigger dog."

"Good idea," I said, relieved.

Back at the house, she continued to ask me questions. "What are you looking for in a dog?" she asked, filling in the form that would match me with my future partner guide dog.

"God, this is like online dating," I said, laughing nervously. "Do you have any dogs that look like Chris Hemsworth?"

The assessor laughed. "Afraid not. But we do have some shaggy blonde Golden Retrievers. Do you have a preference in regard to the breed?"

"I'd quite like a German Shepherd," I said, thinking it wouldn't be as approachable as a cuddly golden Labrador or retriever, which suited me. I didn't fancy the idea of me and my dog being the centre of attention. "But I don't mind really, I'll have whatever is suitable." I knew that the wait for a guide dog could already be long and didn't want to reduce my chances of a match.

* *

One day in June 2018 I got a call from the Guide Dogs training centre. "We've got the perfect dog for you," the man said. It had been more than two years since I'd first joined the waiting list and I was so excited – as well as nervous – that I wasn't able to finish my breakfast.

"He's a golden retriever called ..."

"Tuna? What sort of name is that for a dog?" I thought to myself. "I don't want a dog called Tuna. How stupid would people think I was if they heard me calling for Tuna in the park? They'd think I'd lost my mind!"

Then I realised I had misheard; the man was now explaining how "Tudor" had originally been matched with an 80-year-old blind person in Devon, but it hadn't worked out.

"Tudor was too slow for them," he said.

"Great," I thought. "What does that say about me? I'm less active than an 80-year-old!"

It was arranged that I would spend two weeks getting to know Tudor in Bristol, as this was the city where he had been trained. I was put up in a hotel in the centre. Throughout the hour before my first meeting with Tudor, I paced the large room. "What if he doesn't like me?" I thought. "What if my smells are all wrong?" There are many stories about dogs not trusting certain people. What if I was one of these people? This really was like internet dating!

When Tudor entered the room, his tail gently wagging, I realised all my fears were for nothing. "Pleased to meet you, Tudor," I said, grinning like a fool. He stopped at a respectful distance and I could just about see, through my pin spot of sight, a pair of lovely dark brown eyes.

Every day, I met up with Tudor and his trainer to work with them. At night Tudor slept in my room so we could bond. I listened to the soothing sound of his snoring, the odd whimper as he dreamed in his sleep.

The guide dog training programme is really quite amazing. All the puppies are bred at the Guide Dogs National Breeding Centre in England. Volunteers train them during their puppyhood, and then at the age of 12–16 months old, they start their specialist training at a number of centres across the country.

In 20 weeks the trainee guide dogs are taught to a super-high standard of obedience. They learn not to jump on people or furniture and to come back straight away when they are allowed to run free, off their leads. They are taught to be aware of traffic, stop at kerbs and guide their owners safely across roads. They lead their owners onto buses and trains, all the while avoiding any obstacles and hazards that they come across along the way. They also know how to spot hazards above them such as low, overhanging branches that a blind person could walk into. I was impressed when I found out about this last skill. It was something I had never stopped to think about before.

As a new owner I had to learn too. I needed to know what commands to give Tudor to make him move where I wanted to go. I learnt how to look after him, taking him for regular toilet breaks and lots of exercise. I was warned not to overfeed him, as Labrador retrievers are well known for eating everything and anything, and to make sure he had plenty of regular exercise outside when he wasn't working.

I also needed to understand the difference between "harness-on" and "harness-off". Tudor, like all guide dogs, is trained to know that when I put on his guide dog harness with its metal handle he is focused and working, and when I take it off it's his time to relax.

Once we had got to know each other, it was time to take Tudor home to meet the family. I wondered how he would fit in, as my family had always had smaller dogs such as Yorkshire Terriers. I didn't need to worry – Tudor was the perfect gentleman.

"Isn't he gorgeous," everyone said, cooing over him, like he was a newborn baby or a new boyfriend.

"Look at those eyes. So soft and gentle," my Nan said. "And look at the size of those paws; they're bigger than a Yorkie's head." She tickled the golden, curly fur on Tudor's chest, her bracelets jangling. "You can tell he loves the attention," she continued, "the silly sausage. Oh look, he's showing us his belly!" I couldn't see anything at all that day, but I knew exactly what he'd be doing: rolling over onto his back with his paws in the air and the biggest stupid grin on his face. This, I realised, was one of his favourite poses as he waited for someone, anyone, to rub his belly.

"I think he's fitting in quite nicely," I said to my Nan.

Now he had settled, it was time to take him out for the first time, just me and him. My hands shook as I put on his harness. I hadn't been out on my own in years. I was petrified of crowded cities and struggled to even cross a road. With my track record of falling over without warning, and Tudor's size, 35kg of solid canine power, I was afraid that he might pull me over in his eagerness to guide me.

But there was no putting it off. I had to face my fears and try. Our first trip was to my local gym, which was only a couple of streets away. Before losing my sight, I had loved to go swimming. I hadn't done any exercise for years and I was putting on weight – I could feel my clothes were becoming tight.

With the harness on, Tudor was a different dog. Whereas before he had been rolling around and bouncing playfully, now he was sat upright, waiting for my command. "Forward, Tudor," I said. I held onto his handle and he walked calmly out of the door with me at his side, and led me to the gym. My nerves disappeared. Even with the sound of loud traffic coming at me from the roadside, I felt safe.

At the gym, a personal trainer called Keirra showed me around the equipment, while Tudor sat quietly, watching and waiting. "You've got yourself a gym buddy!" said Keirra, laughing. Now Tudor and I go two or three times a week and he sits beside my personal trainer while I exercise.

One of the things I hadn't bargained for when I became a guide dog owner was the amount of extra stuff I have to carry. Gone are the days when I could go out with just a small handbag for my lipstick and phone. Now I have to carry a full backpack with Tudor's bowl, food and water, treats and toys he can chew if he gets bored, his identity card and his medical book, just in case of an emergency. It's like having a baby, but one that returns the care I offer.

**

With Tudor to guide me I have done things I would never have dreamed of. For example, I had never been on an aeroplane. So when an old friend from university invited us to Edinburgh, I packed two suitcases, one for me and one for Tudor, and booked a flight. Tudor had his own seat on the plane in the space next to mine. When we took off, my stomach tightened with fear so I stretched out my hand and gently stroked his neck. I did all right after that.

I have conquered my fears and travelled around the country visiting cities like Brighton, Bath, Glasgow and Bristol. The two of us also took a train to London to join a mass Government lobby to campaign for better access for disabled people, a cause, not surprisingly, that interests me personally. So now Tudor can add activism to his many achievements.

When he's out of harness, Tudor is the fluffiest, silliest clown. He loves to run and chase his frisbee. He especially loves going for long walks along the beach with his furry friend Jackie, a retired guide dog. Jackie is a yellow Labrador and was only seven when her owner passed away. She was too old to be retrained, so she lives a life of semi-retirement with her new adopted "dad" in Swansea. Jackie's owner helps me to take Tudor for runs on the beach as I'm always afraid I'll lose him, his fur being the same colour as the sand.

**

A guide dog, I have discovered, is a great way to meet

people too. Strangers come up to me all the time saying, "Your dog is so pretty, can I say hello?" Sometimes I don't mind; other times when I'm in a hurry, it can be frustrating. "Of course you can," I'll say through gritted teeth, my foot tapping the ground.

There's a whole etiquette around how to behave around working guide dogs. I have a sign that I sometimes have to put up which reads:

"Meet Tudor.

He is a working dog.

We know he is gorgeous but please do not call his name or get him excited.

He needs to remain focused at all times to do his job properly."

Sometimes it works, but there are many people who just can't help themselves. I work as a freelancer with advertising agencies, and volunteer with the Royal National Institute of Blind People (RNIB). In work meetings it can sometimes be annoying when people just want to talk about Tudor.

"Look at his little face!"

"I bet Tudor's got something to say about your proposal."

"Oh, I just want to take him home with me!"

"Look," I'll say. *"Can we just talk about work, please?"*

Tudor is also better than any dating app, which are not great for blind people, it turns out. Whenever I've tried to use an app, I haven't been able to see what anyone looks like and find myself swiping just anyone. So I gave up on that. I only started dating again after Tudor came into my life, and having him by my side has been wonderful for meeting people. I never have to buy my own drinks. Whenever I go on dates I am clear with people about my sight loss. Although I can't see Tudor, I'm fully aware everyone else can.

One Friday, I went on a first date with an accountant with a deep West Country accent. He seemed nice enough, but halfway through our meal, he started moaning about the food. Then the service. Then the music that was playing. I felt Tudor sit bolt upright beside me and then heard a low grumble coming out of him. It was as if he was saying, "Don't waste your time on this loser."

I promptly made my excuses and left.

**

Since Tudor came into my life, all the anxiety and panic I faced from being on my own has disappeared. When I come into a room and he backs into me with his bum, bashing his long, fluffy tail against my legs, I feel comforted. When I give him a doggy back massage, all worries melt away. He sits upright, waiting for me to throw him his toy, and I don't feel alone in the world.

Tudor's not just my eyes, he's my soul mate. A diva

golden retriever! Together I hope we can travel the world, and not just in my dreams.

Instagram @tudortheguidedog

Hoola's special story time

The reading dog that is making reading fun for dozens of young children

By Grace Vobe

"We have a very special guest in school today," the head teacher announced to the assembled children. A buzz of excitement rippled around the school hall as 60 young children tried to guess who was behind the curtain. Who could it be? Was it a pop star? A football player? A YouTuber?

"Please give a warm school welcome to Hoola," the head continued as I walked onto the stage.

The children's eyes lit up when they saw Hoola, my pet whippet, by my side. Some children clasped their hands together in a display of visible excitement. "I love dogs *so* much," I heard one little boy say to his friend in a loud whisper.

"Hoola is going to be our school reading dog," the head explained. "Once a week, Hoola and Grace will be visiting and four children will get the chance to read to her."

"Me, me, me!" said a blonde girl, stretching her arm in the air.

"Hoola will be working when she is in school," the head continued with a smile, ignoring the girl. "So please respect her and take care. You are not allowed to crowd around Hoola or stroke her without first asking permission. Don't run or shout when she is in the classroom or corridor. If your name is called out, you may choose a book and go to the reading corner to read to Hoola. Now who would like to come up and stroke her?" the head asked.

Sixty small hands shot up in unison.

**

I had been looking forward to this day for months, ever since I had signed up for the Burns By Your Side (BBYS) reading dog scheme in 2016. Hoola and I had been walking around the Pembrokeshire Show when I first saw the Burns Pet Nutrition Foundation's stand. The company, started in 1993 by a vet called John Burns, had just launched Burns By Your Side as part of its charity work.

"What a fantastic idea," I said to the woman on the

stand. She explained how they were looking for suitable dog owners to join up and train their dogs to visit schools and help children who struggled with reading.

It made perfect sense. Dogs are kind and compassionate – I could remember many times when I had had a stressful day or felt anxious, and after a couple of minutes of stroking Hoola on the couch I'd felt much better. A dog doesn't judge or sigh and look at its watch when a child makes a mistake. Why wouldn't a child want to read to a dog?

I went online to find out how to apply.

"Anyone with a well-behaved dog over the age of 18 months can apply to be a Burns by Your Side volunteer," the website said. "Your dog's temperament and behaviour are very important when working with children." They were looking for "some very special volunteers" who enjoyed working with children and could volunteer to visit a school or special educational unit once a week or every two weeks. It said: "Certain levels of obedience and behaviour are required from your dog but full training will be given."

The more I thought about it, the more I realised that it would not only be good for children to read to Hoola, it would be good for me too.

At the time, I was fed up of people asking me what I did for a living and having to say, "nothing!" There were times when I was almost tempted to make something up. "Oh, I'm a veterinary surgeon" or "I do freelance photography". Anything other than "nothing".

The fact was, for 20 years I'd had a successful career as a Personal Assistant in London. But that all came crashing down one morning when I was walking to work and a cyclist collided with me. My head hit the concrete floor and that was it – the life that I knew, that I had built, was over. I was left with severe brain injuries and had to learn to walk and talk again. Everything I had worked for disappeared. I moved back to west Wales to be close to my family. I could no longer work as I was suffering from Chronic Fatigue Syndrome, which causes extreme exhaustion, and Fibromyalgia, a condition that makes my whole body scream out in pain.

It was my doctor who first suggested I should think about getting a pet dog as walking would make me feel better. "Are you joking?" I said to him. "I can barely get out of bed. How am I going to manage walking a dog every day?"

But then along came Hoola, a whippet puppy, and everything clicked into place. Loving and intuitive, Hoola was a huge boost to my mental wellbeing. The first time I took her for a walk, I felt the familiar pain in my muscles, but I didn't let it stop me. I was too busy watching Hoola soak up the world, her skinny tail wagging as she sniffed lamp posts and greeted passing people. A whippet puppy was the perfect pet for me. I was smitten.

I signed up for the Burns By Your Side scheme, and over the months that followed Hoola and I attended a series of workshops and training courses. These sessions were designed to train Hoola – and me – to meet the behaviour standards needed before we could be matched with a suitable school. Luckily, Hoola was a well-behaved dog to begin with, but there was still much to learn. Once qualified, I went through all the legal checks before I could become one of the growing number of BBYS (Burns By Your Side) volunteers working with school children across west and mid Wales.

** **

Once the school assembly was over, Hoola and I went to our reading corner. I had bought Hoola a new, fluffy bed for her school work and set it down in between two cushions. The teacher introduced us to the four children who had been chosen to read.

"But I can't read in English," a girl named Carys whispered, looking as if she would burst into tears.

"That's fine, you can read a Welsh book," I told her and she instantly relaxed. Carys took her place next to Hoola and started reading her Welsh story book. She flew through it, almost word perfect, peeking at Hoola shyly between sentences. At the end of the session I suggested she should bring two books the following week. She did and once again read both Welsh books almost perfectly. The week after, she did the same. I was beginning to think that maybe she came from a Welsh-speaking family and wasn't able to read English books.

For the fourth session, Carys turned up and had forgotten her book. "No problem," I said. "We're here when you're ready. Go and get whatever book you want to read." Off she trotted, reappearing with her chosen book.

To my surprise, she proudly announced, "I've got an English book," and settled down, positioning the book so that Hoola could see the pictures. Very quietly she began to read. When she finished the first page, she looked over to me, pleased with herself.

"'Hoola really likes that you can read both English and Welsh," I said, trying to encourage her. "She thinks it's very clever to be able to read in two different languages." A broad smile spread across Carys' face and she lifted her head with pride, before returning to her book. Seven pages later, she turned to Hoola and said: "My Gran is going to be so proud of me because I've never ever read an English book before." She reached out and ruffled Hoola's fur. "I can't wait to go home and try some of my English books."

I tried to cover my smile with my hands but it was too big to hide. I was overcome with pride and elation.

"I don't know how you did it," her teacher said to me. "We'd tried everything to get her to read English. She wanted to but for some unknown reason, she wouldn't." She spread out her hands in bewilderment. "It's amazing," she said. "Now another world of possibilities and adventures has opened up to her through books."

"That's the magic of reading dogs," I said, smiling, happy that my dainty little whippet and I had made such a big difference.

**

Over the years we've worked with many children in our local school, spending each term with just four pupils. Some of the children don't want to show that they are struggling to read a particular word, so I'll say, "Show Hoola the word". Then I lean close to Hoola so she can tell me the word. This works well with the younger children. For older children, whose reading age is lower than their actual age, Hoola is really good at choosing the book that is right for them. "I think Hoola would like you to read this one," I'll say, handing the child a book. And the child is always happy to read the book Hoola has chosen. Maybe they feel that they are doing her a favour?

If I notice a child is nervous or struggling to start reading, I'll say, "Don't read the words. Hoola doesn't need the words. Let's just look at the pictures." Without the pressure, they start reading. Quickly their confidence grows and when their time is up, I have a hard job telling them to stop.

One morning we were introduced to a new boy, who took one look at Hoola and shied away. He clutched his reading book across his chest like a shield. From the frightened expression on his face, I could tell he would rather be anywhere else in the world than here with us.

"This is Lucas," his teacher said. "His mother wants him to read to Hoola because he doesn't like dogs." Lucas glanced at Hoola fearfully, his mouth going down at the sides.

"You come as close or far away as you want," I gently persuaded Lucas. "Hoola is very friendly." This was Hoola's cue to cock her head to one side, looking at the boy with her gorgeous, melted chocolate-brown eyes. "She wouldn't be allowed to come into school if there was any danger of her biting you."

Lucas didn't seem convinced. Perhaps I shouldn't have mentioned 'biting'. He maintained a safe distance, eyes fixed on Hoola, who just stretched out on her bed. When his 15-minute time slot was over, he rushed out. I wondered whether we would see him again. The following week, Lucas turned up. This time he stood closer. The week after, closer still. Eventually he plucked up the courage to hold out his hand and offer Hoola a treat, the sleeve of his jumper pulled tight to cover his skin. In the weeks that followed, he grew confident enough to sit next to Hoola and stroke her. By the end of term, he was waiting at the school gate with his book and would lie down next to Hoola.

"I can't believe the difference in him," his mum told me later. "He's been scared of dogs ever since he was attacked as a toddler. If he saw a dog in the street he used to freeze in sheer fright. I don't know how you did it, but now he can walk past a dog without shaking. Thank you. Thank you. Thank you."

"It was a pleasure," I said, feeling Hoola's tail thumping my leg as she wagged it beside me.

I'm equally surprised at how intuitive Hoola can be. She seems to know just what each child needs. With some she lies still and listens, allowing them to touch her all over, but with others she physically interacts with them, giving them a gentle touch of encouragement or placing her head in their lap.

Mason was a whirlwind of a six-year-old. He had attention deficit hyperactivity disorder (ADHD) and was a bundle of pent-up energy. Hoola just knew how to make him calm, without any encouragement from me. As soon as he sat down next to her, she leaned against him and rested her head across his legs. He was so fascinated by the dog that he remained still, not wanting her to move.

"How did you do that?" teachers ask. "I've been teaching for 30 years and I've never seen such a transformation in a child."

"Don't ask me, ask Hoola," I'd respond, scratching her behind the ear.

**

As well as working in our local school, Hoola also listens to visually-impaired children once a month. Organised by our local council and hosted by the Burns Pet Nutrition Foundation, a group of children meet up with other children who have similar needs. They then take it in turns to read to one of the two dogs at the session. Alongside some other volunteers, we have been visiting this session for over a year and it has been a pleasure to see the children develop in their confidence and reading ability.

**

There is still a lot we don't know or understand about the academic effects of animal-assisted therapies. Researchers at the University of Wales Trinity Saint David (UWTSD) have been carrying out studies to explore the impact of the Burns By Your Side project. The schools involved all reported how the children have responded well to having Hoola and reading dogs like her in schools.

What I *do* know is that the positive effects on the children I have witnessed have been startling. These days Hoola and I even get recognised on walks. Just the other day a woman came up to me and asked, "Is that Hoola who goes into the school?" When I said yes, she patted me on the back and gushed, "Well done you, it really is amazing what you do. The results have been incredible." It turns out she was a supply teacher who had witnessed the difference we had made to some of the children at her school.

In a world of technology, I love that Hoola and I are part of a project that is sparking the joy of reading in reluctant readers. What started out as a literacy aid has become so much more. It has had a positive effect on my confidence and given me a sense of self-worth and purpose.

**

I was out walking Hoola one chilly Sunday. We were in the woods, following the river, and as always, Hoola walked obediently by my side. I was passing a woman who looked familiar to me. She stopped and said, "Is that you, Grace?"

She was an old friend from school, someone I hadn't seen in a long time. "So what do you do with yourself these days?" she asked.

I felt the old fear. But then I looked at Hoola and my

heart swelled. I don't do 'nothing' any more.

"I'm a Burns By Your Side volunteer," I told her, smiling proudly. "And I absolutely love it."

Medicine doesn't always come in a bottle

The therapy dog that sparked a viral internet dog sensation and helped a terminally ill child

By Jamie-Louise Wallace

Harvey screamed, a prolonged, agonising cry that cut deep into my heart. Every muscle in his small boy's body was clenched in pain as he kicked out with his bent legs. He was reacting to one of the nurses who was trying to replace a feeding tube down the back of his nose and into his fragile body. This wasn't just any tube – it was the lifeline that kept him fed and nourished. Without it, his body would shut down. The more the nurses tried, the louder he screamed. His body started shaking in a fit. He was in so much pain and the medical staff had given him everything they could.

"Can't we just get the dog back in?" I begged.

"Get the dog, get the dog!" a senior nurse shouted, her cheeks red with stress.

Nico arrived, all black and fluffy and ready to work. He jumped onto the foot of Harvey's bed. Harvey calmed down immediately. Nico crept closer to Harvey, curling up next to his legs and giving his toes a cheeky little lick. Harvey's stress melted away and where before he had been tense and uptight, he was now relaxed. He closed his eyes and drifted off. For the first time in months, he slept without the need for medication. The nurses looked at him with slack faces. "I can't believe it," said one of them. "I just can't believe it." It was a miracle.

**

We had only met Nico earlier that day. Harvey and I had been having a particularly bad day. We had been hoping to go home, but then the hospital staff delivered the bad news: we were going to have to stay a few more days.

"We need to go home," I sobbed. Watching my first-born child in agony, knowing there was nothing more that could be done, was putting me and the rest of our family under so much stress.

Harvey had been at the Noah's Ark Children's Hospital for Wales in Cardiff for seven months. During that time, I had remained at his bedside, watching the monitors and machines that fed him and helped him to breathe.

"Harvey has complete gut failure," the doctor had told me. "His body is no longer taking in nourishment. We've done all we can." I knew then that we had to prepare ourselves for the worst. He had a rare condition called intestinal pseudo-obstruction, which meant the part of his body that was in charge of pushing food through his body was no longer working. He was only 11.

**

Harvey had been in and out of hospital his whole life. When he was born he was no bigger than my fist. He looked like an alien, all grey with too much skin for his tiny body. Doctors didn't give him much of a chance from the start. He spent the first two months of his life in an incubator. Being the little fighter he was, he pulled through.

Up until he was nine months old, I thought he seemed pretty normal, if a little small for his age. I was a first-time mum, so I didn't have anything to compare him with. But as he got older I realised that the "Mmmmmmm" he kept mumbling was never going to form the word "Mam".

In the years and months that followed, Harvey had a

series of health and development issues. He was diagnosed with about 30 different conditions. He couldn't talk, he couldn't walk. When he was three, we realised that he couldn't swallow food either, and he was fitted with a 'PEG' tube which was fed directly into his stomach. He would need this tube for the rest of his life.

**

When the doctors first told me they could do no more for him in the spring of 2019, I just wanted to leave the hospital and never come back. I needed to take him to a safe place where he could be surrounded by the people and pets he loved, away from the medics and the bleeps of machines.

"If only I could bring Chance in to see Harvey. It would make everything so much better," I said. Chance was our two-year-old labradoodle. A cross between a standard poodle and a golden Labrador, he was a giant of a dog. He was full of energy and fun, but always gentle with Harvey. Whenever Harvey was having one of his screaming fits, just seeing Chance with his kind, daft face and fluffy, waggy tail seemed to calm him.

Throughout his life, Harvey had been surrounded by animals. He loved them. He was always at his happiest when animals were around. When Harvey was born, we'd had a black and white border collie called Lucy. It was Lucy who alerted us when Harvey first stopped breathing. She stood over his cot and howled and howled. That's when we found out that Harvey had epilepsy, on top of all his other problems. Who knows what might have happened if she hadn't alerted us? I loved watching Harvey and Lucy playing together. She would follow him around and chase the lights from his toys. Harvey's giggles filled up the room. They were inseparable.

*

"OMG, I think there's a therapy dog on the ward today," said one of the hospital managers, clapping her hands in excitement. She was in charge of organising events for the children and their families and just happened to be on our ward that day. "Let me go and check," she said, rushing off.

Moments later, she came back, looking quite pleased with herself: "I've spoken to the dog's owner on the phone. We've missed them today but she says she'll bring Nico back in tomorrow, just to see Harvey. I've also spoken to the nurses and they've said it's all right for Harvey to go and see the dog. How awesome is that?"

It turned out that Nico the cockapoo had been visiting the Noah's Ark Children's Hospital for the past couple of months. His owner Emma belonged to Therapy Dogs Nationwide, a charity which arranges for pets and their volunteer owners to visit places such as hospitals, schools, care homes and prisons to bring comfort to those in need. Emma had seen an appeal asking for help in giving the hospital's young patients and their families some fun activities to do to take their mind off their illnesses. She regularly visited the hospital wards, bringing Nico, and the children who were well enough could go down to the communal hub room to stroke and play with him.

With permission from medical staff, it was arranged that we would take Harvey down to the hub room the following morning to see Nico. It was going to require some serious effort, getting him down there, but I was determined to give Harvey the chance to have some doggy playtime. We made a bed up on the floor of the communal room. With the help of nursing staff we brought down all his monitors, feeding drips and oxygen machines. Then we lifted Harvey into a wheelchair and I pushed him down, ready to meet Nico.

I was beginning to wonder whether I was doing the right thing as Harvey looked awful – he was paler than usual. The room itself was hardly a relaxing place for a child with Harvey's conditions. It was close to the hospital charity shop and the communal fish tank, and there were staff and visitors passing by all the time. He was cold and uncomfortable. I could see that he was getting distressed by all the background noises. When I tried to lift him out of the wheelchair and onto the bed, he clenched every muscle in his body. His arms and legs were as stiff as ironing boards. His hands were curled into tight fists. Suddenly he let out a long, loud scream. People passing by turned their heads: you would think I was trying to kill him.

Then in trotted Nico, wearing his bright yellow Therapy Dogs bandana, and I swear in that moment it was as if Harvey had been swapped with another child. The screaming stopped and his eyes lit up.

"Would you like to see Nico do a trick?" Emma asked Harvey, taking a treat out of her pocket. On command, Nico sat up and begged, showing off the white blaze of fur on his chest. It looked like he had a napkin tucked in his collar. He took the treat and sat back down. Harvey's smile grew wider.

"Why don't you give Nico a treat?" Emma said to Harvey. I lifted Harvey onto my lap and together we held out a biscuit. Nico sniffed Harvey's hand, and the tickle of his wet nose on Harvey's fingers made him laugh. Ever so gently, Nico took the treat and looked straight into Harvey's eyes, as if to say "thank you".

"Isn't Nico lush," I said to Harvey, stroking Nico. Being a cross between a Cocker Spaniel and a poodle, he was big enough, but not too overpowering. His fur was soft and fluffy and he smelt of dog shampoo. He was like a living, breathing, prancing teddy bear.

For almost an hour we sat in the room with Nico and during that time it felt as if all the pain and stress of the previous few days had never happened. Harvey was totally relaxed. His usual grumbles and cries were replaced by laughter and happy sighs. As we said our goodbyes, I wondered if Emma would mind if I kept Nico until it was time to go home.

"If you want us to come in again, just call," Emma said as we parted. She couldn't have known she would be back that same night.

** **

Seeing the way Nico lifted Harvey's spirits, the staff at the Noah's Ark Children's Hospital charity took to social media and posted a video of them together. The post read:

> "Can you help put a smile on Harvey's face? Dogs are his favourite thing ever so we want to put together a video of yours saying hello to him. Harvey, who's receiving palliative care, had a tough day yesterday but this is him laughing at one vid he had. DM us your #HoundsforHarvey."

Within minutes we were inundated as strangers from all over the world started sending in their videos. There were Labradors playing pianos, huskies in Alaska singing, Dalmatians running on beaches, West Highland white terriers springing through the snow and mastiffs bouncing on trampolines. A black Labrador introduced himself as "Dylan the villain" and in a little girl's voice, admitted stealing socks off the radiator. A sheepdog sang along to George Ezra. Some dogs trotted around with big sticks in their mouths, others chased balls. Some just curled up in their beds and snored. Lots said, "I love you, Harvey."

In just two days more than 1,000 videos flooded in. It was overwhelming, but lovely at the same time. We showed them to Harvey to keep him smiling during his last days in hospital.

When we finally got back home to Merthyr, the videos kept on coming. Newspapers and magazines across the world reported on it and the Hounds for Harvey campaign went viral. Celebrities and sports stars joined. The Malone family from the TV programme *Gogglebox* posted photos of their Rottweiler Dave, while Spiderman actor Tom Holland shared photos of his dog Tessa.

It wasn't just dogs. People across the world posted photos and videos of all their animals. We had elephants in Thailand, baby tigers in India, monkeys in Africa. One little boy from California was deaf and allergic to most animals so he sent a photo of his pet fish. Another little boy, who was also deaf, said hello to Harvey by teaching his dog sign language.

We streamed all the videos to the TV next to Harvey's bed while his dad, myself and his younger brother and sister took it in turns to sit and watch them with him. They kept us laughing for hours and hours during the months of pain that followed. They also helped to take his mind off the horrible job of receiving regular medication. Even Chance the labradoodle seemed to enjoy them, tilting his head as he watched the screen or looking behind the TV to see where the animals had disappeared.

The staff at the Noah's Ark charity were amazed by the way people around the world had come together in one common cause to make Harvey happy. Everyone was so supportive and warm. Someone commented: "It's nice to see something that doesn't cost anything, takes less than five minutes and puts a smile on so many people's faces."

Added together, we probably had a million videos. We posted updates showing the positive effects these acts of kindness were having on Harvey. Out of all of them, his favourite was the first time he met Nico, because he could see himself in it. He would watch it with a big grin on his face and point at the screen.

**

Towards the end of May 2019, the Hounds for Harvey campaign was still going strong, but Harvey's health was weakening.

On June 1, I sat down with my tablet to write the most difficult post of all.

> "I've sat here and thought of so many different ways to write this, to make sure I get it right but I just can't. Yesterday afternoon our outstandingly brave warrior and amazing boy took his last breath. We wanted to let you know as you have been amazing xx"

Once again we were overwhelmed with videos, but this time the people and animals who had posted funny photos were now passing on their messages of condolence. "RIP, Harvey," they shared. It was awe-inspiring, knowing that Harvey had affected so many people he'd never even met. In a way I felt bad for everyone. I didn't want to make anyone else as sad as I was. But even during those darkest moments, the video of Nico at Harvey's bedside made me smile.

**

Harvey's friendship with Nico left a lasting legacy for other children at the Noah's Ark Children's Hospital. Having seen the positive effect it had on Harvey, staff realised that there were many other children who could really benefit from time with a therapy dog, but for a variety of reasons couldn't leave their wards.

And so, provided with a clean sheet to prevent the spread of germs, Nico was allowed to visit many children in their beds and the results were amazing. One girl with cystic fibrosis was so ill she had been in isolation for months. Medical staff were trying to get her back on her feet, but she was so depressed she shut down, refusing to do anything. On the day when she had agreed to try to walk, Nico turned up as a surprise. As she stood up from her wheelchair, Nico ran to her. She reached out and grabbed his lead. With Nico and Emma at her side she walked down the corridor, much to the amazement and delight of her family and nurses.

One child in intensive care opened his eyes for the first time in days when he felt Nico lay down beside him. Another, a girl who couldn't see or hear, moved her hand and wiggled her fingers to touch Nico when she felt him jump up on her bed.

Having a visit from a therapy dog quickly became the most popular activity for children and their families at the hospital. Nico is like a big, comforting teddy who gives children and their families a break from the hospital routine. Stroking and petting him provides important relaxation in highly stressful situations. For some children it helps them miss their own pets just that little bit less.

For many others, it is the thing that stands between agony and peace, that ushers a smile in an otherwise despairing face. Just like it did for Harvey.

*

Following the success of #HoundsforHarvey we have joined a new campaign on social media – #Joinourjungletribe – to help other seriously ill children and their families at the hospital.

Harvey spent more than half of his final year on the Jungle Ward at the Noah's Ark Hospital, where we got to know all the staff and other families. Although the care was first class, the facilities there need modernising to bring it up to the standard of the other wards.

The Jungle Appeal was launched to raise £64,000 to build new facilities, including a sensory room where children like Harvey who have special and complex needs can go. We want every child on the ward to have the chance to spend time with a therapy dog, if they want to, in the privacy and comfort of a dedicated therapy room. It will be such a help for everyone, including the staff busy giving the medical care and the families worrying about their children's mental health and wellbeing. I hope that Nico and other therapy dogs like him will be a big part of the new facilities on the ward.

We can't bring Harvey back, but we can make sure his

memory lives on. I think sometimes we take our pets for granted, but it's amazing to see how much of a difference having a dog around can make to a child's happiness. It certainly did with Harvey. Nico showed us that the best medicine doesn't always come in a bottle.

The dog from death row with so much love to share

The Romanian street dog that found love and affection among care home residents

By Ann Cooper

A video popped up on my Facebook timeline – a skinny, scared dog peeking out from behind a tatty wooden fence. In a second she was gone.

"Come on, Blue," came a woman's voice with a heavy Eastern European accent, and the dog reappeared. She had light honey-coloured fur and a dark nose. She ran in a circle, bowed down low, then leaped up as if inviting the person behind the camera to play. Her paws flailed in the air and her tail wagged furiously.

The film had been posted online by the Laika Fund for Street Dogs, a charity which rescues and rehomes street dogs around the world. There were three dogs in the video, all rescued from the streets of a Romanian city. The open-air pen where the timid dogs were sheltering was small and made of dirty old bits of wood of all shapes and sizes, nailed together. In the far corner there was a box where the dogs made their shelter. The floor of the kennel was bare earth. It was hardly paradise, but it was a heck of a lot better than where they had come from. It was also better than where they might be heading.

Blue, it seemed, had been named because of a blue cast in one of her eyes and the mask of steely grey fur on her face. She was a cross between a husky and who knows what else. Her fur was short and cream-coloured, flecked with a blue-grey stripe that ran down her spine to the tip of her long, strong tail. Her over-sized paws were almost white, and matched a streak down the right hand side of her muzzle. Two patches of light fur above each eyebrow made her look like she was frowning. She had dark, almost black eyes that made my heart melt. She was so pretty.

Some of the street dogs are vicious, difficult to retrain, and too dangerous to live in a home with other people and pets. But in Blue I saw kindness and a willingness to learn new things from the way she was interacting with her rescuers. As I watched the video, I knew that I wanted to give this frightened but friendly dog a home in west Wales.

** **

Blue, I learned, had started her life as a young puppy growing up on the streets of the Romanian city of Constanta. From a very young age she had to fend for herself, finding scraps of food wherever she could. She wouldn't have seen the metal noose of a catch-pole coming until it was too late and the wire was tightening and cutting into her neck. She was dragged on the end of the pole, wriggling and trying in vain to break free as she was thrown into the back of a dog-catcher's van.

Romania has had a problem with stray dogs ever since the country was freed from its Communist dictatorship in the late 1980s. It's said that as people's priorities changed, dogs were no longer important; many were turned out on the streets, creating a stray street dog society, which Blue had been part of. To rid the streets of the problem dogs, people were paid to catch them and take them to kennels where many ended up being destroyed. For the lucky ones, there were charities such as the Laika Fund, working to give these animals a future.

Blue was one of the lucky ones.

I sat down at my computer and began composing an email to the Laika Fund for Street Dogs. It read: "I have seen your appeal and would like to offer Blue a 'forever home'. I live with my husband on a small farm in Carmarthenshire in west Wales. We own fields where she can run and there is farmland and woods nearby where she can have plenty of walks. I am experienced with dogs and training and have owned dogs all my life. I have five other smaller dogs, four cats, several horses and chickens, and I would give her a good life."

I hit send and crossed my fingers. Soon I got the response I was hoping for. The charity arranged to send out an inspector to check that my home was as safe and suitable as I had said. Once I had passed all the checks, they prepared Blue to travel. After she arrived in the UK she was put into quarantine for four days before I could collect her. Once she had been checked over by vets and they were satisfied she didn't have any dangerous, infectious diseases, I was able to collect her. I drove to the south of England to meet her at the charity's collection point. I had already decided that I would rename her Lady.

Lady seemed very confused and afraid at first. As I carried her towards my car she took one look at the vehicle and tried to struggle free. She was probably having flashbacks to the day she was dragged from the streets of Constanta and thrown into the back of the truck. And God knows how it had felt for her, travelling 1,500 miles across Europe.

"Come on," I gently coaxed her, using bits of tasty chicken to tempt her.

After some persuasion, she finally relaxed enough to climb into the back of the car, where a deep, soft bed was ready for her. She had never had the luxury of a bed and, at first, was nervous about lying on it. It would be another two years of persuasion before she ever felt comfortable enough to jump into the car on her own.

** **

When I arrived home with Lady, I had to introduce her to our cats. I wasn't sure how she would react as I didn't know if she had ever seen one before. For their first meeting I put Lady into a cage in the middle of the room and allowed the cats to investigate. Being curious creatures, they crept up to the cage and peered in through the bars. Lady fixed them with a stare.

"Be nice," I said, and she wagged her tail.

I opened the cage door and one of the more forward cats stepped up to her. She rubbed her face against Lady's in a display of trust and Lady allowed them to touch her.

"Good girl," I said. "I think we're all going to get along just fine. One big happy family."

Every day was a new experience for Lady. Even something as normal as grass was strange for her. She had never seen it before and took some time to realise that she could walk on it without hurting herself. Watching her grow from a scared, shivering creature into a confident, calm companion, I knew I had done the right thing in rescuing her.

**

As Lady's confidence grew, so did our bond. I volunteered for a charity called Carmarthenshire Therapy Dogs, a group of volunteers and dog owners who visit lonely people in their homes or in care homes or hospitals. Some of the people we visit have mental health issues. Some have learning difficulties, others have long-term illnesses like Alzheimer's, which causes them to forget people they used to know. They can even forget how to do simple things like dressing themselves. But they like to talk and stroke animals; it gives them comfort and makes them feel less alone.

"I think you could be a fabulous therapy dog, Lady," I told her one afternoon as she was lying across my lap, having her tummy tickled.

I took Lady to my local vet to assess her behaviour and suitability as a potential therapy dog. They checked to see how she would react to sudden movements and strange noises. They banged empty tins together. Lady stayed calm. Compared to the noises she heard on the streets and in the kill shelter in Romania, I'm guessing there was little they could do to scare her.

** **

Our first therapy visit was to a small care home in Carmarthenshire. Before we set off, I bathed and groomed Lady, making sure she was clean and presentable for the new people she was going to meet. To show everyone that she had a job to do, I put on her green and yellow therapy dog coat and clipped a blue 'working' lead onto her collar, and off we went.

On arrival at the home, we were met by one of the carers, who led the way. There was a corridor lined with doors, leading to the bedrooms of the elderly residents. We heard loud hacking coughs and the hissing of oxygen machines coming from inside as we passed by. Lady glanced for a moment, and then walked on calmly.

"Good girl," I said, as we walked. "There's nothing to be afraid of. That's only Jack. It's his lung disease that makes him cough so much."

The carer stopped at one of the open doorways along the corridor. "Sit," I said and Lady obeyed.

"Lady the dog has come to visit us today," the carer announced. "Would you like to see her?" We had to ask first as not everyone likes dogs. Some people might be allergic to fur and we wouldn't want to make them ill.

I led Lady inside the room, where an elderly man was sitting upright in his armchair. He looked so lonely and empty, but he smiled when he saw us. It was almost as if someone has switched a light on behind his eyes.

"Sit," I said again and Lady placed her bottom on the floor next to the chair where the man was sitting. He stretched out his hands and touched her fur with his thin, frail fingers. "Would you like to give her a treat?" I asked, handing him a tiny biscuit. The gentleman held out his hand and Lady took the biscuit from him ever so gently, like I'd trained her to do. After a while I could see the man was starting to get tired. "Time to go," I said. We said our goodbyes and moved on to the next room.

Some of the people we visited were so poorly they had to stay in bed. Therapy dogs are not supposed to jump up on beds. The elderly often have skin as thin as paper and there's a real danger that a dog's claw could injure them by accident. I felt this was so unfair. So, after a bit of research I came up with the idea to make Lady a pair of blue woolly socks to wear, so she couldn't hurt anyone.

Altogether we spent over an hour at a time visiting people in different care homes. Wherever we went, smiles followed us around. For some of the elderly, who were no longer able to remember the things they used to, they seemed to go back to a time when they were younger and had dogs of their own. They would see Lady and huge beaming smiles would transform their faces. Maybe they were remembering their childhood dogs, or the puppy they'd bought their child.

* *

Whenever Lady saw me getting her green and yellow therapy dog coat and blue socks ready, she knew we were going on a visit. She would start wagging her tail and sit by the door in eager expectation.

One of Lady's favourite people to visit was Margaret. Margaret was 98 years old and hadn't been able to walk for many years. For the past two years, she hadn't even been able to get out of bed. Every day, her carers would go into her room to wash her, brush her hair and give her meals, which were mashed up as she could no longer chew normal food. Yet Margaret knew what day we visited and was always ready for us, sitting up in bed with a treat ready for Lady.

We arrived one Saturday to find Margaret smiling, with her dog biscuit ready. I laid Lady's blanket onto Margaret's bed. That was her signal to jump onto the bottom of the bed, as I'd trained her to do. She crept up the bed on her tummy, ever so gently. Halfway up, she stopped and rested her head on Margaret's belly. Margaret held out her hands and stroked Lady.

"Isn't she a clever dog?" I said to Margaret.

"Clever dog," Margaret mouthed back. I looked over at Margaret's carer and saw tears glistening in her eyes. This was the most Margaret had spoken in over a year.

**

I've lost count of the amount of free cuddles Lady has given out over the two years we've visited care homes. All the smiles she has received. The memories she has evoked. I believe everyone should be entitled to a therapy dog if they want one.

**

We work well as a team, me and Lady. As well as our work with her as a therapy dog, I have also trained Lady as an agility dog, and together we have won lots of prizes at shows including a Bronze Agility Award. We even qualified for the 'Discover Dogs' competition finals at the most famous dog show in the world, Crufts, when I entered Lady in the finals of the Friends for Life competition for her work as a therapy dog.

Lady loves to be loved. After such a cruel start in life, I feel like she has returned the kindness by helping others. It has restored her faith in humans and she has so much more love to give.

"We are soul mates," I often tell her, kissing the top of her cool nose. And Lady returns my affection with a big, wet lick.

My dog's sixth sense saved my son's life

By Hannah Stokes

"But Muum," said Johnny, sat at the kitchen table. "If you get me a dog I promise I'll walk it and feed it every day and I'll clean up all its poos. You won't have to lift a finger, I swear."

Sighing, I filled the sink with dirty plates. "That's what all teenagers say," I said. "But it's always the parents who get stuck with all the duties once the novelty's worn off."

"But *Muuum* ..."

**

I suffer from epilepsy, a condition which affects my brain and causes me to have fits when I get over-tired. I also cared for my 90-year-old father and was concerned that a dog might knock him off his feet. It didn't feel the time was right to take on the extra responsibility of looking after a dog.

By the time Johnny reached the Sixth Form, he had given up on hinting and asking. He had finally accepted that we were never going to get a pet, so he put all thoughts of a dog out of his mind.

One morning, we were in the kitchen again, chatting, when Johnny flinched. He screwed his eyes up tight and punched his forehead with the palm of his hand.

"What's wrong?" I asked, concerned. This was not normal behaviour for him.

"Just a headache," he replied.

"What do you mean, 'just a headache'?"

"It's nothing, I get them all the time," he said dismissively, as if it was the most normal thing in the world. "I just wait for them to pass from excruciating to severe. No biggie." He gave me a wry smile.

But I was concerned. As well as the headaches, Johnny was sleeping for an abnormally long amount of time. As a mother of two teenagers, I knew it was 'normal' for teenage boys to spend all day and night in their bedrooms. But with Johnny it was different; he was sleeping for 18 to 20 hours out of 24 most days. While awake he was in constant pain. Sometimes when he was talking to me, he would close his eyes and his legs would shake with tension, caused by unbearable pain. I persuaded him to go to see the doctor, but every time he went, he'd come home saying, "The doctor says it's probably a migraine."

I started to keep a sleep diary, noting down the number of hours Johnny slept in every 24. Armed with this, we visited the doctor, who referred him for a brain scan.

A week later we were called back to the hospital. The doctor looked grim. He asked us both to sit down, tapping his fingertips against the desk. "There's no easy way to say this," he said. "Johnny has a brain tumour. I'm recommending an emergency operation." I gripped Johnny's hand, my stomach turning. It was a week before his 18th birthday.

The tumour was on his pituitary gland, which sits just behind the nose and controls many other glands in the body. Before the surgery, the medics sat us down as a family and explained what could happen if the surgery went wrong. The tumour was at the base of the brain. They warned that there was a risk he could die under anaesthetic or end up brain-damaged. In my mind, a brain tumour was a slow terminal death. It grew until it killed you. There was no real choice – the tumour would grow. So a date was set for surgery.

As we left the hospital following Johnny's diagnosis, my daughter Tara whispered to me, "Don't you think we should get a dog? Johnny's always wanted a dog. Maybe now is the time."

"At this point," I whispered back, "if Johnny asked for a herd of elephants, I'd say yes."

"Yeah, don't do that," she said. "Think of all the poo."

So we contacted our local dog rescue kennels, who sent someone out to meet our family and check that our house and garden were safe to give a dog a home. Once approved, we went off to the Greenacres rescue centre to choose his first pet. Johnny couldn't have known it at the time, but his life would depend on which dog he chose to bring home.

"Look at her," said Johnny, pointing at a large young Labrador cross. "I like how pretty she looks."

I read the sign screwed onto the mesh gate: "This is Pippa. She is 18 months old and she is a bundle of energy!"

"She's rather big," I said. "She'll need a lot of walks."

"I like her," he said, smiling.

And so Pippa bounded into our lives, sleek, black and long-legged. She had been dumped at the kennels by her former owners who no longer wanted her because she had chased sheep while off her lead. This made no sense to me as it was the owner's responsibility, I thought, to keep any dog on a lead when around sheep. However, their loss was our gain, as in no time Pippa proved to be a valuable addition to our family.

"Look, Mum, she loves me," Johnny exclaimed, as Pippa planted her paws onto his lap and licked his nose. "She doesn't give anyone else kisses."

A cross between a Labrador and a Dalmatian, Pippa had the soft dark eyes of the former mixed with the elegance of the latter. Dalmatians are an ancient breed, known for their hunting and guarding skills. In past times, Dalmatians were popular with noblemen and would trot alongside carriages, leading fire-fighters in their horse-drawn fire carriages to the scene of a blaze. Black Labradors are a breed most suitable for training, whether as guide dogs for the blind, therapy dogs for the disabled or sniffer dogs detecting drugs at custom borders and airports or bombs in war zones.

I knew all this, of course, because Johnny kept telling me. He had Googled the breeds, reading countless articles about them. "And guess what else," he would say, his face lit up by the laptop screen. Smiling, I would listen to the next factoid. Pippa, luckily, had inherited the best characteristics from both breeds. Loyal and intelligent, she was keen to obey and eager to please and had an outgoing, friendly personality.

Within a short time Pippa and Johnny became the best of friends. If Johnny was scared about his impending brain surgery, he tried not to show it. She would nuzzle up to him and repeatedly lick his nose. Johnny would laugh, rubbing her ears and head and encouraging her to continue. It was lovely to see.

**

The day of Johnny's surgery arrived and we packed our bags and headed for the hospital in Cardiff. Knowing that we would be away for some time, we arranged for Pippa to stay with friends. It was a worrying time for everyone, Pippa included. My friends rang me, telling me how she would cry in the evenings. "I think she misses Johnny," they said. "It's almost as if she senses something. Like she's worried about what's happening to him."

It was a long, terrifying wait as the surgeons performed the operation. We paced the waiting room, too sick with fear to eat anything, glancing at the clock every couple of minutes. No parent can possibly imagine how it feels, to wait for the outcome of an operation that means life or death. Finally, the head surgeon entered the room. He was smiling. "Good news: the surgery was a success." I barely heard his words. The smile had been enough.

After several weeks, Johnny returned home to the warmest welcome anyone could expect from a pet. Pippa was beside herself. Her tail was wagging so much she almost knocked me off my feet. She was so excited to see us all again, but it was Johnny who soaked up most of her attention. She circled around him, rubbing her strong shoulders against his knees and head-butting his hands and legs. If she could talk, I'm sure she would have said: "Don't you ever leave me like that again!"

**

Three months passed and life went on as it had done before the tumour. Johnny locked himself away in his bedroom, determined to catch up on the school work he had missed out on. While he worked, Pippa would lay across his feet like a sleek, furry foot-warmer.

One afternoon, Johnny and I were sitting on the sofa watching TV when Pippa carefully crept up onto his lap and started licking his nose furiously.

"Stop it, Pippa, I can't see the TV through your head," he said, gently trying to move around her. But Pippa wouldn't be calmed, she kept licking and licking. She seemed certain that there was something behind Johnny's nose. I panicked. She hadn't done this since he'd had the tumour cut out. Throughout the evening and into the night, Pippa continued to nuzzle her nose in Johnny's face, licking his nostrils, near where his damaged pituitary gland lay.

I had heard, thanks to Johnny's googling, amazing stories of how dogs could be trained to sniff out illnesses in human beings. There's a charity called Medical Detection Dogs that trains dogs to do just that. I'd also heard how dogs are being trained to sniff out Parkinson's disease, and how others can tell if a person has malaria just by smelling their socks.

A dog's sense of smell is forty times more sensitive than a human's, or even the most advanced man-made instrument. So it makes perfect sense to train them to smell the chemical differences in the human body that are caused by human disease.

Fortunately, the doctor shared our faith in Pippa.

"Your dog was absolutely right," the doctor said as he delivered the results of the second scan. "The tumour is growing back. It's very small and compact at this stage, and we may not have picked it up so early if your dog hadn't noticed."

Johnny was referred back to hospital for a second round of brain surgery. Again, the tense long wait in the waiting room, the constant glances at the clock. And again, success. Johnny made a full recovery and went to university in Swansea, as he had always planned. Following graduation he qualified as a heart technician and went to work in a hospital in north Wales. I was so proud of him.

**

Pippa stayed at home with me and the more time we spent together, the more I realised that she was so much more than a pet.

One morning, I took her with me to the shops to buy a loaf of bread for my morning toast. We had only been out of the house for five minutes, when, without warning, she planted her bottom on the pavement and refused to move any further. I tried to give her a gentle tug on her harness, but the harder I tugged, the more she refused to move. "What's got into you, you silly, obstinate thing?" I said. She looked up at me, panting, her bottom still stuck fast to the ground. Frustrated, I turned around and headed back home, without the bread.

Minutes later, when we were back in the safety of our home, a wave of extreme tiredness swept over me. I had no choice but to go to bed. I was going into the first stage of a build-up of 'petit mal' seizures. This is what happens when I get over-tired or stressed. The fits are also triggered by flashing lights or pain and can be dangerous, especially if I were to black out while outside and hit my head on the hard ground. Because of this risk, I am not allowed to drive and have to walk everywhere, which can be hard work when I have to carry heavy shopping bags home from the supermarket.

Once rested, I reflected on what had happened. Had Pippa sensed something and tried to warn me? Was she trying to tell me I needed to go home and rest?

At other times when we were at home together,

Pippa would repeatedly paw my legs and rub her nose in my face for no reason. At first, I thought she was just being a nuisance and tried pushing her away. But her insistent behaviour was often followed by me having a repeated seizure, which could be the trigger for a full-on 'grand mal' attack.

One of the most unusual incidents happened one sunny afternoon, when I took Pippa to visit a friend. We had a leisurely 30-minute walk to the farm where she lived and spent a lovely afternoon in the fields, helping to exercise her horses. Later, when we were sitting in her kitchen drinking tea, Pippa started nuzzling against my body, batting me with her paws. I didn't take any notice and carried on sipping my cup.

Then Pippa turned her attention to my friend. She pushed her nose in her face, and then looked through the open back door to the yard, where my friend's car was parked. She continued pacing back and forth, nudging my friend, and then started running towards the car. I wasn't aware of what was going on as I was on my way to having a full seizure. Luckily my friend recognised what Pippa was trying to tell her. She helped me into her car and drove us both home.

Later, when I was safely tucked up in my bed, I thought about what had happened, amazed by Pippa's thought process. She must have thought, "I can't get through to

Mum. Mum's not going to walk home safely. We can't walk that far home. I need somebody to take her. I need my Mum's friend to take her in the car. How do I get her to understand?"

It may sound like something out of a Lassie film, but without her intervention, who knows what might have happened if I had passed out on the road on our long walk back home?

**

Pippa and I are a team now. Wherever I go, Pippa is by my side. I know that if Pippa is happy and relaxed around me, I am going to be all right. I can get on and do things without the fear of having an epileptic fit. She has given me the confidence I need to live a fuller, more active life. Although she has never been formally trained as a medical alert dog, I trust her intuition. She senses when I am getting tired and warns me to either go to bed or take medication. She is my own personal alarm system.

Wherever I go, whether out shopping or visiting friends for coffee, Pippa walks beside me wearing her medical alert dog harness. Together we have undertaken advanced behaviour training, which allows us to volunteer as a reading dog with the Burns By Your Side project. Once a week we visit our local library, where she sits quietly and listens as children with special needs read to her. She is so calm and well behaved.

I am so fortunate my son chose to bring Pippa home from the rescue kennels on that day in 2014. Black dogs are quite often the last ones to be adopted from rescue centres. Whether people think they are unlucky, or just because they don't look as cute as lighter coloured dogs, who knows? I often ask myself, was it luck that caused Johnny to fall in love with Pippa's gentle face and pretty eyes? Or was she attracted to my son because she sensed we needed her? All I know is that it was the best choice he ever made.

Some nights, I'll sit with Pippa, watching TV, my hand on her warm head, and I'll remember all the times that Johnny pestered me for a dog. And all the times I said no, worrying about how I'd manage to look after a dog with my condition. "Turns out, it was the other way round!" I'll say, stroking her. "*You* look after *me*. And you saved my son's life. Not bad for an unwanted rescue dog, eh?"

The greyhound that
never gave up

How an injured racing dog provided
relief to stressed-out students

By Hayley Donovan

I first met Zed at a sanctuary for retired and injured racing dogs. It was summer and I wanted to give a rescue greyhound a home.

Zed caught my eye. He was a handsome boy. He had deep, smoky grey fur and eyes as black as coal. When he saw me he twitched his long snout and limped forward to greet me, his long sinewy tail waving like a flag. As he moved, I could see his back right leg was bandaged up to his hip.

"That's Zed," the manager at the Greyhound Rescue Wales sanctuary told me. "He shattered his back leg in a race and was brought to us." She furrowed her brow. "Lame dogs can't win races."

"That's horrible," I said, "to just drop a dog once it's no longer any use."

"Can't agree more," said the manager. "As you can see, Zed here is on the mend, but it will take a while for his shattered bones to heal. He's looking for a 'forever home'."

I looked at Zed and tickled the white patch of fur under his chin. He was a stunning dog all right. He could be a perfect companion for my other dog. But I wasn't in a position to adopt a dog that might need ongoing vet treatment, so I said goodbye to Zed and kept looking.

**

Six months later I got a call from the Greyhound Rescue Wales sanctuary. Would I be willing to foster Zed in my home? It turned out that I wasn't the only one put off by his broken leg. He had been in the kennels for six months, being overlooked every single time.

"Would you take him in just for a couple of weeks?" the manager begged. "Get him used to living in a home. Teach him to be comfortable around the noise of TVs, vacuum cleaners, washing machines – that sort of thing?"

I agreed. And that was it. Within a couple of weeks, it was obvious that Zed was going nowhere.

My husband had always wanted a rescue greyhound, ever since the day we came across a group of volunteers on a charity dog walk in the woods near our home in Swansea. The dogs on the walk were so well-mannered and the people from Greyhound Rescue Wales, who looked after them, were friendly and devoted to helping the breed.

At that point, we already had two elderly rescue dogs at home, a Bedlington terrier and a whippet, which looked like a miniature greyhound. When, a couple of years later, the time came to say goodbye to them, we took in our first rescue greyhound, Gem. She was three years old and ever so shy. Everything in life seemed to frighten her. Her quiet personality meant she didn't have what it takes to win races. She was slow and always came in last, and so of course she was put up for adoption.

Zed was quite the opposite. He had been an outstanding racer in his short career. He was owned by one of the UK's top champion greyhound trainers and travelled to racing tracks all over the country. Flying along the track, he won race after race for his trainer until the day he was injured – and that's where Greyhound Rescue Wales stepped in.

Injury is one of the most common reasons that racing greyhounds are retired. Every year thousands of dogs like Zed end up unwanted because they can no longer run as fast as they used to. If they can't win and make money for their owners, they can be disowned. Many get put to sleep – not always in the kindest of ways. The lucky ones get rehomed. That's where charities like Greyhound Rescue Wales can help. Over the last 25 years it has helped more than 3,000 dogs, Zed included. Alain Thomas, the charity's founder, believes "no dogs should be put to sleep", and set up the Last Hope Fund to pay for treatment to help fix injured dogs and give them the hope of a long and happy future.

The fund is named after Last Hope, who was a racing greyhound left for dead on a mountainside in south Wales in 2004. When Last Hope could no longer race, his owner paid someone to 'destroy' him. That person left Last Hope on a mountain, lying on a pile of rubbish with a hole in his forehead and his ears cut off. He was found by a walker who called in the RSPCA and was taken to a vet, where he was put to sleep, humanely.

After that horrific case, Alain and the GRW volunteers decided they would do all they could to make sure such cruelty would not be allowed to happen again. The Last Hope Fund covered the costs of treating Zed's broken leg and in return, he became the poster boy for its fundraising activities.

I looked upon Zed as a bit of a sad case. Although

the broken bone in his back right leg was mending well, he had a toe missing on his hind left leg, the result of another racing injury. During the six months he was in the sanctuary, they also found another problem: his spleen, the organ which makes blood cells and fights infections, had also been damaged sometime in his racing life. So the vets decided to remove it as most dogs can manage quite well without it.

In spite of all his problems, Zed immediately made himself at home with our family. Outgoing and friendly, he just wanted everyone to like him. Whenever I sat down, Zed would jump up onto the sofa beside me and stretch out, laying his paw across my lap. And that's how he would fall asleep, living up to the greyhound stereotype of a couch potato.

Gem was nervous of him at the beginning. He would bound around her in circles, wanting to play, and she'd look at me, her tail quivering between her legs, as if to say, "Help me, Mum!" But gradually, she warmed to him, and soon they were good friends.

**

Every morning I take Zed and Gem out for a run in the park before I head off to work. They always race off with a sudden burst of energy. But, being typical greyhounds, they soon run out of steam. That's the thing about racing greyhounds, retired or otherwise – they have no stamina. The average greyhound race is only around 30 seconds to a minute long, so any longer than that and they just give up.

Some of the ex-racing greyhounds also have what is called a 'high prey drive'. It's down to centuries of being bred to chase and kill small animals, or 'lure'. The lure is an artificial animal that travels ahead of the dogs on the racing track. Some of the most successful racing greyhounds can be a nightmare to take out walking – if they catch a glimpse of a rabbit, squirrel, pigeon, cat or even a small dog, they'll chase after it. Gem and Zed might chase the odd squirrel but, luckily for me (and the squirrel) they are never fast enough. The squirrels always scamper to safety up a tree way ahead of the dogs.

**

One morning Zed was chasing a bird across the park when my heart stopped. He let out the most blood-curdling, high-pitched scream of agony. Any greyhound owner knows about the Greyhound Scream of Death. Once heard, it's never forgotten. Being sensitive souls, the slightest thing like a minor scratch or even stepping on a slug in the grass can set them off screaming. I had been told about it by another greyhound owner and had laughed, saying, "Surely that's not a thing!" But here I was, hearing it for the first time.

I panicked. Running to where Zed was lying, I saw that he had fallen into a pothole and hurt his leg. Carefully I helped him up, all 34kg of sinewy, athletic greyhound, got him into the car and rushed off to the vet, where he stayed. That evening when we took him home, he walked stiffly into the house and onto his bed.

"I don't know, there's something that doesn't seem right," I said to my husband.

"Maybe he just needs a good rest?" he suggested. But I wasn't convinced.

The following morning we got up but there was no Zed to greet us. I knew something was wrong. I hurried downstairs to find him lying on his bed, looking up at me with his sad eyes. He tried to get up but his legs wouldn't move. He was totally paralysed. We took him to a specialist vet who suspected that a blood clot from a previous injury had found its way to his spine, causing the paralysis.

"We can operate, but we might have to remove his leg if he is ever going to walk again," the vet warned.

"Do what you can for him," I told them. Many dogs manage to get around on three legs and if that's what it was going to take to get him back, that was OK with me.

After 18 days in the vet hospital and a £13,000 bill, we were allowed to take Zed home. We arrived to collect him and were met by the saddest-looking greyhound I had ever seen. The fur on his neck and back had been shaved off. A veterinary nurse was holding him up in a sling with a handle on top and straps around his belly. They had managed to save all four of his legs, but when he tried walking, his back leg shook and wobbled to one side. It was as if he was getting used to being on four legs all over again.

"You need to hold him like this when you walk him, so he can build up the strength in his leg," the veterinary nurse explained. She was using the handle on top of Zed's harness to support and guide him.

"Just walk him little and often and make sure you support him. Keep him on a short lead. We don't want him to start running and damage his leg again."

That was easier said than done. But my husband and I persevered and gradually got him walking again.

**

During Zed's recovery, as he grew stronger walking on his injured leg, I got a call from Greyhound Rescue Wales asking if Zed was ready for a new challenge.

"We're looking for volunteers to help stressed out students," Alain explained. "If you think Zed is up to it, we'd love to have him on board. He could be a great inspiration to students."

I was sceptical at first. What could a wobbly-legged

greyhound have to offer students? And what would I talk to them about? I had left school at 16 and worked in a garage.

**

The first Study Aid session was held in the library of the Students' Union at Swansea University in January 2017. It had been organised by a member of staff who also turned out to be a huge dog lover. The dog petting sessions, she explained, were intended to be a welcome break from studying, to reduce stress for students during exam times.

I arrived with Zed and Gem and joined eight other dogs and owners from Greyhound Rescue Wales and other rescue charities. Zed and Gem settled down on their beds in the corner and waited. "I wonder if this will help?" said one of the owners. "I could have done with something to help with my exam stress when I was in uni."

"I think it seems like a barking idea," I said, and luckily, everyone laughed.

Outside the room, we could hear the excitement as students lined up waiting for their turn to meet the dogs. The event had been advertised on the students' Facebook page and had become an instant hit. Up to 80 students signed up, so they were given tickets and set times so that the dogs wouldn't be overwhelmed.

The first group of students entered, nervous at first. A dark-haired young woman edged her way towards where Zed was taking a nap. He opened one eye. I could see him thinking, "What's in this for me?"

"What's your dog's name?" the young woman enquired.

"Zed," I said, holding out a corner of a Bonio dog biscuit. "Would you like to give him a treat?"

Quick as a flash, Zed was up on his feet, sniffing the student. She smiled, stroking his head. In that moment, a bond was formed. The girl was in her third year studying history. She was thousands of miles apart from her family and worried that she would not pass her exams, disappointing her parents. She had a pet dog back home in China and was missing his cuddles. "He is so cute," she said. "Sometimes he slept on the end of my bed and kept my toes warm." She looked up at me. "What sort of dog is Zed?"

I told her all about greyhounds, how they were bred to race and what happened to them when they could no longer run. She told me about how stressed she had been feeling recently, how she slept only four hours a night and revised for so long that she would start seeing double. While we talked, Zed sat up and allowed the student to stroke the top of his head. As he relaxed, he rolled over onto his blanket ever so slowly. The young woman followed his lead, lying down on the floor beside him. Head-to-head they lay there in silence.

"This is your last minute," the organisers called out. Already we could hear the voices of the next group of students gathered outside, waiting for their turn. They were being briefed on what to expect and how to behave around the animals.

Reluctantly the young woman got up from Zed's blanket. "Nice meeting you," she said, rubbing Zed's head in a final goodbye, and she walked out with her head held high, more relaxed and confident than she had been when she came in.

✷✷

Our dog Study Aid sessions have become the most popular of the student wellbeing events. We visit every December and June as these are peak stress times at universities. Some of the students who come to meet us have dogs at home, and during the pressure of exams they long for their home comforts. When they walk into the sessions you can see their faces light up as they look around to see which dog they want to fuss. Seeing how much fun students have and how happy they are when they leave makes it so worthwhile.

Students love to hear Zed's story. "Whatever life throws at him, he just gets up and carries on," I tell them.

I love to see how he is inspiring students to deal with whatever life throws at them too.

It's hard not to be happy when you see a dog wagging its tail at you.

If the stories in this book have inspired you to find out more about the work of therapy, assistance and support dogs and their volunteers, here are some places you can go for more information.

Burns By Your Side/Burns Foundation
Website: burnspet.co.uk/charity   www.johnburnsfoundation.org
Telephone: 01554 891915

Carmarthenshire Therapy Dogs
Website: facebook.com/Carmarthenshiretherapydogs/

Greyhound Rescue Wales
Website: greyhoundrescuewales.co.uk
Telephone: 0300 0123 999

Therapy Dogs Nationwide
Website: tdn.org.uk
Email: enquiries@tdn.org.uk
Telephone: 07840 994 003

Guide Dogs Cymru
Website: guidedogs.org.uk
Email: Cymru-mt@guidedogs.org.uk
Telephone: 0345 143 0195 (Cardiff office)
             or 0118 983 5555 for general enquiries.

Noah's Ark Children's Hospital Charity
Website: noahsarkcharity.org
Telephone: 029 2184 7310

Acknowledgements

Thank you to all owners and their 'working' therapy, assistance and support dogs for sharing their stories.

Thank you also to the staff and volunteers at Burns By Your Side, Greyhound Rescue Wales, Guide Dogs Cymru, Therapy Dogs Nationwide, Carmarthenshire Therapy Dogs and the Noah's Ark Children's Hospital charity.

All the stories are true, but some places and names have been changed to protect the identities of those children and vulnerable adults.

Congratulations on completing a 2020 Quick Read.

The Quick Reads project, with bite-sized books, is designed to get readers back into the swing of reading, and reading for pleasure. So we sincerely hope you enjoyed this book.

Got an opinion?

Your feedback can make this project better. Now you've read one of the Quick Reads series visit www.readingwales.org.uk or Twitter @quickreads2020 to post your feedback.

→ Why did you choose this book?

→ What did you like about it?

→ What do you think of the Quick Reads series?

→ Which Quick Reads would you like to see in the future?

What next?

Now that you've finished one Quick Read – got time for another?
Look out for the other title in the 2020 Quick Reads series – *Hidden Depths* by Ifan Morgan Jones.